Every Seven Years You Change
Does your personality change too?

Tony Crisp

Contents

A response to reading Every Seven Years You Change,

Hi Tony- You probably won't remember me; I used to come to Combe Martin in the 1980's on Richard and Juliana's Intensives Psychotherapy workshops... I remember fondly how we all enjoyed your and Hy's wonderful cooking!

Just wanted to say that as I approach old age (nearly 70), welcome changes are happening. Firstly, I'm accessing information I never knew I had, mainly evident in my enthusiasm for University Challenge on TV where I will often find the correct answers to questions on disparate subjects, they just seem to pop out of my head without consciously thinking which, in addition to surprising me, are sometimes not even guessed correctly by any of the eight panellists!

Secondly, synchronous-type occurrences are becoming more frequent. Things such as suddenly thinking of a friend I've not thought about for maybe weeks, only to have him or her then call or text me less than a minute later!

Also, the wider, world view you write of is becoming stronger in me, where I get a (intuitive) sense of the world at large, a strong feeling for the multitude and mass of humanity, and principally its collective suffering, which is a much more expansive experience than previously I've had most of my life i.e. my own small world and its restricted boundaries.

I've enjoyed, as I get older, the growth of my intuition, and celebrate its development in contrast to left-hemisphere mental (?) attributes such as intellect, objectivity, etc. I'm both fascinated and pleased to find your writings on these subjects, and more, on your website. It feels appropriate that I have come across your site at this time in my life.

Thanks for sharing all your wisdom on the site.
Best wishes. P

Every Seven Years You Change
Most cells in your body is renewed over a period of time
Does your personality change too?

ARE you the same person now that you were fifteen years ago? In fact, are you the same person you were just seven years ago? Most of us have heard the old saying that every cell in the body is changed over a period of seven years; but recent investigation has uncovered facts of far more significance to us as human beings. This concerns the emotional, physical and mental changes that seem to occur in approximate seven-year intervals.

Of course there are no fixed boundaries and so one may achieve these levels of maturity at any period of our life. so what follows are simply the general changes you may find. Rudolph Steiner, the great teacher of Anthroposophy said that the seven-year cycles continue throughout life, and are of the utmost importance to doctors, teachers, psychiatrists and the social sciences. Without some smattering of these changes it is difficult for anyone to understand the relationship of any given individual with his or her environment.

So I have tried to summarise what Steiner and others have said about the cycles. Before the definition is started, I feel it is important to say that as humans, in fact as any life form, we are creatures of great polarities. Or as the philosopher Erwin Goodenough said, "A book on love, loyalty or justice would gain little but pedantry by starting out with a concise definition of the term. Only as we describe the various conflicting elements associated with such words can we finally arrive at a meaning that includes these complexities; for important matters we understand, not as we simplify, but as we tolerate the paradoxical."

One of the great paradoxes of our lives is that we constantly go through such enormous such massive changes every day. Each of us is immersed in a 'river' of constant change. If you think about it you have been carried, pushed, impelled by this current as you were moved through babyhood, childhood, teenage and adulthood, and there are more stages of growth beyond adulthood. And as we pass through these changes we died to our old self in order to change to the new. It is the current of Life. This current then carries us on through old age and through the gates of death. All the time we are faced by decisions, and each decision directs us on a different path, helping to create our future.

Daily we also pass through an extraordinary change that we often take so much for granted we miss the wonder of it. The change occurs between sleeping and waking. For most of us being awake is when we most fully feel ourselves. See **Lucidity**

Compared with this sleeping is a period during which we lose any focused awareness of being an individual, and we sink into what is generally called unconsciousness — the lack of personal awareness. This swing between waking and sleeping can be seen as the extremes within the possibilities of our experience. Sleeping and waking are the polarities, the North and South Poles of what we can confront. In quite a real sense we can say there is nothing beyond what is included in those polarities. But there is an enormous difference between waking experience and the experience of dreamless sleep. Yes, one can have an experience of what is considered deep unconsciousness. In waking we have a sensation of time, of being in a locality, of separateness and even isolation. But at the other end of that polarity we have a sense of timelessness and non-locality. What was a sense of self merges into an ocean of awareness.

0-7 years

One of the most important of these cycles is the first, from birth to seven years of age. Its importance lies in the fact that it is the beginning of everything, the foundation upon which the later structure will be built. Birth gives individual life to an infant body. Even at birth, this small being already has its given potential of intelligence, creativity and personality. But this potential has to come to terms with its environment, which includes its own body. In a human being we cannot have awareness without consciousness; we cannot have thinking without the tools of thought such as language, concepts or ideas. So during our early years we are largely moved by the instincts of hunger, need for love, survival, protection and support, along with pain and the impact of our environment. All this while we build up the inner, mental structures that in later years will allow us to think, to feel, and to be aware of ourselves as an individual.

The most important of these inputs is that of the unconscious behavioural responses we learn. From the moment you are born, perhaps even prior to that, you are learning, or there are pressed upon you, responses to what you are experiencing. The culture you are born into is a huge ready-made set of behavioural responses. For instance, an Australian aborigine would easily respond to a huge living grub/caterpillar by eating it. This would be a very difficult behavioural response for most Northern Europeans or Americans. As babies we learnt everything from whether you respond to opportunity with fear or eagerness; to love with fear of warmth; to food as a glutton or with healthy appetite.

At birth there is a very different physical and glandular system than in later years. For a start the sexual organs have not developed, meaning responses to sex and sensation are very global. Also the thymus is very large and in later years becomes smaller. It has been said this, in these early years, gives the child a very primitive response to truth, right and wrong, and what later become moral codes. So the child only slowly develops any real sense of social morality. In a way a baby is a wild animal, and only slowly develops 'human' qualities.

But something so mysterious happens to us during this first seven years that once done it can never be fully undone. The Roman Catholic Church recognises this by saying that if they can have the first seven years of a child's life, that is all they need to insure a lifelong influence. Napoleon also observed that as the twig is bent, so the tree will grow. This is borne out by seeing the cases of children who have been lost and brought up by animals during these formative years. Even with the best tuition they never learn to become a self aware personality as we know it. Time is a mystery to them, and even though their brain size and function is normal, they never approach the usual capabilities that education gives to modern women and men.

So, in the first cycle we pass through an incredible process of learning. This includes motor movements, speech, relationship to ourselves and to our environment. And that means learning a vast amount about what is useful, entertaining or harmful; about what responses we get from others, and developing habits of response that may be difficult to change in later years. We learn a sense of personal awareness and move toward becoming an individual. In other words, we learn to say "I" and know what we mean.
.

The learning of language is like a powerful computer program that gives us the ability to develop an identity and self awareness. This is shown again by children reared animals. Language also adds limitations which we can overcome if we recognise them. See **Programmed**

Steiner also says that during this first stage of development the developing inner forces are working to transform the body of the child from one that was inherited from the parents, to one that represents the full personality of the child. See **Animal Children.**

Something often overlooked about the stages of growth are ones emotional age.

From age zero we are completely dependent upon the loved person for our needs, physical, emotional and social. Great anger, jealousy or pain are felt if the loved one relates to anyone else, is lost, or threatens to leave. If we do not mature beyond this emotional age, in adulthood this enormous feeling reaction may also be felt at a time of emotional withdrawal of the partner, even if there is no sign of them withdrawing physically. In the infant and toddler there is a desire for unconditional love and a need to be always with the loved one. In an adult with this developmental level of love, sex may be a part of the relationship, but the main need is a bonded connection. This is sometimes felt as a need to have the loved person want you as much, or as desperately, as you want/need them. Possibly the greatest fear, one that can trigger great anger or an enormous desire to placate or earn love, is the threat or fear of being abandoned.

The point is that certainly in the past, and still today in many parts of the world, abandonment means death. The greatest and most prominent drive in a baby animal is to stay connected with its parent or group. If it doesn't it will almost certainly die. That instinct has been built into us as vulnerable animals for millions of years. The baby cannot help but feel that imperative. It will react with tremendous emotional force, swinging between extremes of placation and murderous rage. In a baby that can simply be noisy, but many adult still carry this 'baby' inside them, and its responses can be tragic for them, or even end in murder. See: **Ages of Love**; **Lifeline of Love**

This is so important, that if during this and the next cycle, any feelings that you were abandoned or lacked love were felt, then you must be aware that you have a huge time bomb that can be triggered in your life.

Adult men and women with that time bomb in them can become painful victims of their desperate need for 'love'. This can happen at any time of life, even the late sixties or beyond.

A woman can be triggered by any signs that a man or woman 'love' them, and they can be so hypnotised by such attention that they become a sexual slave for a man, which when he has finished with her, or she demands a loving and not just sexual relationship, is cast off, often leaving great painful wounds.

A man can equally fall in the same way. So it is important to recognise whether you have been the victim of abandonment, sexual assault as a child, or just unloving parenting. If so, recognise you are very vulnerable when someone takes an interest in you.

Another very important part of a child's life that is barely recognised in our culture is that we all learn enormous amounts in a similar way to how a fox cub learns from its parents – without any verbal communication. Just as a fox cub 'learns' how to hunt from its parents, so we absorb the deeply etched survival strategies of our parents simply by being around them. The process instinctively draws in the survival tactics that perhaps even our parents themselves have never really been aware they live by. In doing this the higher animals learn what cannot be passed on as instinct, what is not 'hard wired' into them. This holds in it a tremendous advantage because 'hard wiring' takes a long time.

So, not only can one have a 'gene pool' from which our body is formed, there is also a 'behavioural pool' acting as a similar resource. This does not so much shape the body, but certainly gives form to the character and responses. But we not only absorb the help attitudes and behaviour of our parents but also the awful strategies many people us to survive.

So if you can develop something of the ability to stand outside of you attitudes that most of us identify as US, see if you can find and assess these deeply buried behaviours.

7-14 years

The second cycle, from seven to fourteen, continues this growth. The concepts and association of ideas and emotions that began in the first cycle begin to be discovered by the child. The physical changes also prepare the growing personality for the next stage. The thymus gland decreases rapidly in size, allowing the development of a sense of right and wrong, and social responsibility. A sign of this physical and psychological growth is the losing of the milk teeth and the emergence of our adult teeth. This marks an entrance into a new maturity.

The child has learned, with the advent of its concepts and developing emotions, to create an inner world of its own. It is a world of heroes, danger and vivid imagination. As the thymus fades, and the sexual organs develop, the personality glides into the turbulent world of puberty and adolescence.

Sometimes it is already evident, even from the preceding cycle, the direction of interest and activity the child will take in maturity. Although for the very observant this might be seen in very early years, it becomes more evident as one approaches puberty.

In all a time of inner expansion. You begin to experience and test abilities in the broader sense of the outside world. You may learn to share and interact, controlling earlier instincts in favour of group dynamics. The habits learned in the first period are now part of the character of the growing child.

Erik Erikson gives his insights into the next phase.

Competence - Industry vs. Inferiority - School-age / 6-11. Child comparing self-worth to others (such as in a classroom environment). Child can recognize major disparities in personal abilities relative to other children. Erikson places some emphasis on the teacher, who should ensure that children do not feel inferior.

Fidelity - Identity vs. Role Confusion - Adolescent / 12 years till 18. Questioning of self. Who am I, how do I fit in? Where am I going in life? Erikson believes, that if the parents allow the child to explore, they will conclude their own identity.

However, if the parents continually push him/her to conform to their views, the teen will face identity confusion.

Intimacy vs. isolation - This is the first stage of adult development. This development usually happens during young adulthood, which is between the ages of 18 to 35. Dating, marriage, family and friendships are important during the stage in their life. By successfully forming loving relationships with other people, individuals are able to experience love and intimacy. Those who fail to form lasting relationships may feel isolated and alone.

Generativity vs. stagnation is the second stage of adulthood and happens between the ages of 35-64. During this time people are normally settled in their life and know what is important to them. A person person is either making progress in their career or treading lightly in their career and unsure if this is what they want to do for the rest of their working lives. Also during this time, a person is enjoying raising their children and participating in activities, that gives them a sense of purpose. If a person is not comfortable with the way their life is progressing, they're usually regretful about the decisions and feel a sense of uselessness.

Ego integrity vs. despair. This stage affects the age group of 65 and on. During this time an individual has reached the last chapter in their life and retirement is approaching or has already taken place. Many people, who have achieved what was important to them, look back on their lives and feel great accomplishment and a sense of integrity. Conversely, those who had a difficult time during middle adulthood may look back and feel a sense of despair.

On ego identity versus role confusion, ego identity enables each person to have a sense of individuality, or as Erikson would say, "Ego identity, then, in its subjective aspect, is the awareness of the fact that there is a self-sameness and continuity to the ego's synthesizing methods and a continuity of ones meaning for others" (1963), Role confusion, however, is, according to Barbara Engler in her book Personality Theories (2006) "the inability to conceive of oneself as a productive member is a great danger; it can occur during adolescence, when looking for an occupation."

14-21 years

This is the third cycle, from fourteen to twenty-one. During it we become conscious of ourselves in a new way, and with a different relationship to life. One might say we become "self conscious." The emotional range expands in all directions, and with this a new appreciation of music, art, literature, sex, and people begins. It is found for instance that at puberty the ability to distinguish subtler tones of colour and sound develops. Besides this the person might go through the difficult struggle of breaking away from home life and/or parental influence. It naturally produces conflict as the person learns some degree of independence. Also, the opposite sex, or sex as an urgent impulse, usually becomes all important as the new emotions pour in upon our personality. See Example 5 for information about facing adolescence.

Because as I write this as I have reached the age of 85 and so have lost most of the glandular and sexual impulses that are incredibly powerful in a teenager. This has led me to have a new view of the range of feelings, many youths experience which gives them a different relationship to religion, relationships, and life's mysteries. Something I have realised through this is that 'falling in love' as it is called is purely a glandular event. It fires enormous stimulus to our emotions and leads us to see certain men or women as wonderful. Of course that is nature at work in us, and if the urge is traumatised it leads to neurotic behaviour. Understanding that we can work with instead of being dominated by it.

All this huge change, as one approaches twenty-one, produces an individual with some sense of social and individual responsibility, or if not that the beginning or a sense of a direction or life purpose. This might not be recognised as such at the time. But it is a time of searching for life purpose, independence, a realization of choices plus a testing of social and personal limitations as well as an awareness of a burgeoning sexuality. As this is a traumatic period of life for most of us, it is also likely to be a time of many unforgettable dreams. See **Exploring a Dream**

The period is a time of adding maturity, dignity and poise to the person. If these changes have not occurred by twenty-one, then the person has in some way not covered necessary aspects of development, and both psychology and the law recognises that they are lacking maturity.

This period is one of great and sweeping changes, sexually, physically, emotionally, morally and mentally. Such enormous changes often do not occur without an experience of loss. In this case the world of childhood is fading, or it might even be torn away, leaving scars. See **Psychological Vomiting**

It is also a time when many new features of the personality have their beginning, i.e. the religious sense, appreciation of the beautiful, etc. Although such things have their beginnings here, they sometimes remain undeveloped until later years. Because of these changes, and because such a lot is being revealed in these years, it is obvious why so much thought should be given to early marriage. Because of one's changing viewpoint, the particular partner one would choose at seventeen or eighteen, is likely to be different to the partner chosen at twenty-one and beyond.

The emotional development at this age is possibly seen as initial uncertainty or clumsiness concerning emotional and sexual contact. It often involves desire to explore many relationships, unless there are forces of introversion or personal and social uncertainty at work. We are still finding out what our boundaries and needs are, and the sexual drive as at full flood. Any partner we have at this time may be loved for ones own needs – rather than out of recognition of who the other person is. Great romantic feelings and spontaneous love which are often difficult to maintain in face of difficulties.

Many women often remain at this age, and search for romantic teenage love dreams their whole life, causing much emotional pain. Men may not move from the very genital phase of this period, so go on a life long search for the next woman's vagina to fill with their dreamed of big penis and great manhood. See **Beware of Love**

Each of us are immersed in a 'river' of constant change. If you think about it you have been carried, pushed, impelled by this current as you were moved through babyhood, childhood, teenage and adulthood. And as we passed through these changes we died to our old self in order to change to the new. It is the current of Life. This current then carries us on through old age and through the gates of death. All the time we are faced by decisions, and each decision directs us on a different path, helping to create our future. And this is a force of growth and change; and is fought like hell by many as we are afraid of such changes, especially getting old and facing death.

21-28 years

The cycle that follows from twenty-one to twenty-eight, can more or less be called a process of enlargement and refinement. It is the period that we mentally and emotionally enter into adulthood. We start to build the foundations of our careers and intimate relationships with a driving energy that we hope will gain us entry and respect in the larger world.

One of the most marked features is the developing sense of discrimination. The faculties of insight, intuition, judgement and understanding begin to come to the fore. The personality softens and begins to mellow. The sparks of interest that were awakened in the previous cycles begin to be developed along more definite lines. The abilities of the last cycle also flourish. The adult emotional age may begin to emerges if one has successfully grown through the previous levels. This shows as a growing sense of recognising needs of ones partner yet not denying ones own. It is followed by an ability to be something for the partner's sake without losing ones own independence or will. One becomes more aware of the issues that colour or influence relationship, and meeting them in cooperation with others. Independence and connection can appear together instead of opposite ends of a spectrum. You move toward becoming caring sexual partners through discovering each others needs and vulnerability.

Sometimes we make people into our satellites in a relationship. We do not see them as themselves, but as someone or something which serves our personal needs or fears. We use the person much as we might use a car, as something waiting to fulfil us. I use the word satellite though because we see the person as someone attached to us, orbiting around us, responding to our signals.

This is really about not recognizing that each person what is unique and different from ourselves. This factor of difference in other people it is of immense importance and underline his a lot of human problems and misunderstandings. Even so, if that is recognised and understood independents and connection can appear together instead of opposite ends of a spectrum. You don't know if it'll water becoming caring sexual partners there are discovering each other's needs and vulnerability.

In this period you will begin to confront the issue that you were either born with, or arose through the challenges and pains of your infancy and childhood. These usually show as the way you handle intimate relationships, whether you can really meet in partnership with the opposite sex, and how you respond to the external world, its challenges and opportunities.

At this time what is revealed may not be and addressed as a personal problem or issues to be healed or re-evaluated. They will be faced more directly later if not dealt with now.

28-35 years

The changes become more subtle as the years pass. The next cycle from twenty eight to thirty-five, for instance, is one where the creative process of mind becomes most active. Researchers and inventors seem to make their greatest advances during these years. It is interesting to note that physical science finds evidence of the reason for this in the fact that the association centres of the brain come to their peak efficiency at about thirty-five years of age.

This is even more interesting when we see that most of the great religious teachers and philosophers came to some vital experience at thirty-five. Jesus, Buddha, Paul, Dante and Jacob Behmen were all in the region of thirty-five at the point of their greatest insights. It would seem then, that if there is an inspirational influence at work in the life, it would possibly reach its peak during these years in and around thirty-five.

Here we take stock of ourselves and the emotional influences that have shaped our body and personality. We begin to determine what is us and what traits we have been pressured by family, peers or society to adopt. Something that we might over look is a long view of our health. In trying to advise people and having myself live a long life there is something I learnt of vital importance, For example my father died and 63 of high blood pressure. He was apparently healthy apart form one medical operation on his prostrate. It was not cancerous. Also my mother gad several stroke attacks and she died from one as did her father.

What has that got to do with you? Your parents gave you the gift of their genetic makeup and it passes on. So my father left me the gift of high blood pressure. My mother

the gift of tendency toward strokes. It is only now in my eighties that

I really understand my and your need to be aware of these hidden gifts. Despite having an excellent diet. 20 or more years a vegetarian and teaching yoga and other healthy practices I still live with high blood pressure and had a real killer stroke. I only survived through the real skill of the surgeons at the Hampstead Royal Free Hospital in London. See **Tony's Experience of Stroke**

So my advice is to check your families health to see what illnesses they suffered or what killed them. Then find out how you can avoid them. Often it is not the regular doctors who advise preventing illness as most doctors usually prescribe what they feel cures the disease not prevent it. For example, Dr. Noakes made a statement to the public in South Africa that the 'normal' foods they ate are the cause of the many illnesses they experience. The normal foods are those manufactured that we eat. The main ones are all products made with white flour that is highly manufactured and is no longer a natural food. This includes many of our staple dietary floods such white bread, pizzas, pancakes, white sugar and white rice.

35-42 years

From the thirty-fifth to the forty-second year, depending upon one's personality and what one's circumstances allow, one begins to feel a new restlessness. In some degree a desire to share whatever one has gained through life with others comes to the surface. Thus we find many successful business men building libraries, or aiding colleges and the arts at this period in their life. What has been developed or realised can be taken to greater subtlety during this period. This is almost like unfolding something, perhaps similar to the way a flower unfolds a bud that has been developing in earlier phases of its growth.

This is when we reassess the results of what we are doing externally in our life. Our relationships, careers, habits and the ways we interact are all put under scrutiny and modified or changed. It's a time of facing up to what does and what doesn't satisfy us.

You may reach heights or realisation and creativity not touched previously. The profound breakthrough of ones innate genius that emerges around this time will no doubt be expressed in some degree. However, whatever is attained or realised will be enlarged and synthesised in later periods.

You are about to enter the most creative period of your life – 35. I see it as a burst that opens in us that colours all the years afterwards. But you need too be ready to burst, like flowers do that are green one moment and then suddenly burst into COLOUR.

42-49 years

In the next cycle from forty-two until forty-nine a major change usually takes place. It is as if one takes all of one's life experience up till this age and begins to digest it, and extract from it new ideals and a new direction in life. There is often tremendous unrest in this period and that following it. The unlived aspects of life cry out to be recognised and allowed. The desire to make a mark in life if it has not already been achieved presses for action here.

At this point it appears to many of us that we have reached the mid point of our life and from here on there will be a decline. Even if this is not so it is often felt very strongly and acted upon in one way of another. People change partners, life directions, and even attempt major personal changes, although these latter may have begun in the last cycle.

Sexual urges are primarily based on reproduction. So in the middle age marriages the man often is seen to leave the marriage to go with a younger woman.

The woman may lose her impulse and passion for sex at this time too. Our society has not built this into its accepted standards, so a great deal of pain and change goes on at this time. The spiritual aspect of this need to be defined and explored. For example, is there an alternative to the reproductive urge cycle in the older male and female?

Also, the emotional age and the maturing of love may at last show signs of an unconditional love. If this is not appearing in small degree, it might be one is still locked in earlier ages. Strangely, many of us maintain the emotional age of a child right into mature years, feeling all the fear of abandonment, jealousy and possessiveness of our childhood. Many divorces and new directions appear around this period. See **Ages of Love**

In these years we move from old stereotypical roles with a new found confidence in our individuality. We are prepared to please our self, rather than society and gain a real understanding of our uniqueness, accompanied by a sense of urgency to express our true self before it gets too late.

I put the following dreams in to illustrate some o f what is met in this and perhaps the next period.

> "I am a mature 40 year old, don't normally dream, and am not unduly fanciful, but this dream has really shaken me. It felt like death. In the dream, my husband and I are at some sort of social club. The people there are ex-workmates of mine and I am having a wonderful time and am very popular. My husband is enjoying my enjoyment. Then he and I are travelling down a country lane in an open horse-drawn carriage. It is very dark and is in the area we used to live in. We come to a hump-backed-bridge, and as we arrive at the brow of the bridge a voice says, 'Fair lady, come to me.' My body is suddenly lying flat and starts to rise. I float and everything is black, warm and peaceful. Then great fear comes over me and I cry out my husband's name over and over. I get colder and slip in and out of the blackness. Then I start to wake up. It takes a tremendous effort, as my body is very heavy. I am extremely cold and absolutely terrified, with a feeling of horror. There seems to be something evil here. I force myself to get up in the dark and go downstairs. Even with the light on I feel the presence of great evil."

The first part of this woman's dream and what she says of herself shows her as an outgoing person, with a happy disposition. She likes people, and they like her; she is probably good looking, and healthy. She feels herself successful at what she has worked, and has left having acquired friends. The relationship she has with her husband is also depicted as one in which pleasure can be allowed within caring independence. Her dream image of herself is therefore created out of her own confidence. Dreams frequently summarise the quality of ones life and the 'story so far' in their first scene.

The second scene is made up of several parts – the journey, the woman's relationship with her husband, the force of nature symbolised by the horses and the countryside, and the unknown seen as the bridge and the voice. To understand what this reveals of the dreamer, look at the vital clues: what she has said about herself and what she felt in the dream. If you strip away images to see what attitudes or emotions are exposed, you can see the forces behind the dream plot. The most poignant statement she makes is in saying, "It felt like death."

If we consider the central image of the dream, the hump-backed bridge, in relation to what she says about her age, the feelings of death's approach make sense. When you approach a hump-backed bridge you climb, but at the very brow, the descent begins. Isn't that a powerful symbol of life? In our younger years our strength, sexuality and ability to meet life with resourcefulness and independence increase, until middle age, when the decline sets in. You cross over – as this woman crosses the bridge – from one type of experience or view of life to another. The passage of time is seen here as the horses pulling her carriage inexorably towards the change.

But the dream's beauty, its depth and drama, are in the voice, and in the discovery of how death 'feels'. They tell us something about women's inner lives, PLURAL. They reveal how, in her prime, a woman confronts change and the view of death in a way few men do. "Fair lady" the voice of change calls, "come to me." And it beckons the dreamer towards a hefty mid-life crisis, asking her to exchange her sexual peak, her firm body, her fertility, for the different perspective of post-menopause. Many women – men too of course – gain their sense of value as a person from their 'attractiveness'.

Losing whatever it is that makes them sexually desirable and socially popular – or fearing that they are losing it – will lead to a significant change in their way of life and their feelings about themselves. This is what makes the dreamer call for her husband. This is what produces the feeling of isolation and terror. A woman needs reassurance and love at this point in her life. She may behave indecisively and deflect the advances of her man through a lack of self-esteem. Fortunately the human personality is resilient. Even though we are reared to identify ourselves with what our body looks like, what it can do, what sex it is, what age it is, and how others react to it, we CAN grow to mature independence without constant reassurance. Some people create these nocturnal horror movies when leaving school or sitting exams. But middle age is just another phase of life, with as much potential for growth and love as any other phase – and as much room for failure. This woman fears what she imagines middle age will do to her. The dream isn't an intuition of her future. Here is a dream from a man in the same age period.

> I recently reached my fortieth birthday and dreamt I was walking uphill. It was quite tough going. When

I got to the top I saw the road on the other side was very steep. I felt frightened of going down it. I looked around and saw that the top of the hill stretched away on each side, so there was plenty of space, like a plateau. I realise that I can walk around and there is no hurry to go down the hill. – John H.

I commented on this dream by saying that before you actually got to middle age you obviously had the idea that it leads directly to a fast decline - going down hill. Your dream corrects this by showing that in fact you have worked hard to climb to a plateau of ability and possibilities that you can now explore. Each portion of life has its rewards, and in fact you depict this period of your life as more relaxed than the first half.

To balance this view a little, if there are still past difficulties to be faced, these will certainly present themselves. But a drive in many people is in some way to actualise themselves, to express themselves in a satisfying way. If we use the analogy of a plant, it is as if they have grown and reached full stature, but for some reason have not flowered and spread seeds. They have not produced fruit.

There is no one way in which people feel or seek this fruition prior to death. But it does become an imperative for many. It may involve receiving or giving love. It might be a need for expressing in one of the arts, or simply in breaking away from habits and roaming the world. The next dream illustrates this theme.

I flew over a farmyard and a large pig saw me and began to chase me as a dog might, but with the sense that he/she wanted to eat me. She chased me snapping and leaping into the air trying to 'get' me.

I felt a bit apprehensive at times that she would get my leg. This lowered my confidence in flying and I began to worry about altitude, and flew over a barbed wire fence and the pig and her young could not follow. I flew low over small trees that were just coming into leaf. They were beautiful soft green leaves. I knew it was autumn and the leaves were only just coming out because it had been a cloudy, overcast summer. I felt the leaves would have time to mature because the sun would be out in the autumn, and the trees would not die.

The dreamer was in his fifties at the time of the dream, and had distinct feelings of something missing from his life. He felt very clearly that the late autumn expressed how he felt, that the best of his life, his fruition had not yet occurred. This was because 'it had been a cloudy, overcast summer.' By this he meant his life had so many difficulties, he had not had a chance to 'flower'. But the dream promised there was still time. In fact 'he actualised' so much from there on.

And here is another dream example showing the same thing.

I am in a bicycle race with many other people. I came to a very long hill. It is difficult and I have to push my bicycle. It takes me until midday. When at the top I meet a lot of family. Then I cycle on, realising that because the road is flat, I can go much further before nightfall than I covered in the morning.

The man was in his late forties at the time of the dream. It shows him feeling as if the first half of his life has been a long difficult climb. His assessment or intuition of the second half of his life is that it will achieve much more, or cover more ground and he will have more human and warm relationships, represented by his family. The bicycle represents his personal efforts to deal with life and his place in the human race; and as it suggests, he can go much further before nightfall – death – than he achieved in the morning of his life. This actually occurred for this man.

49-56 years

In this, and the next cycle from forty-nine to fifty-six, and the periods that follow, the physical changes bring about a mental or spiritual climax. The decline of physical prowess and vitality, forces the person to direct their attention inwards more frequently. Any problems of our personality, such as maladjustment and our repressions, will undoubtedly become more urgent in these years. This reacts upon one's marriage and professional life alike. The problem is that we have to learn to live with ourselves in a new way. We slowly have to adapt to our new-old body, and habits of long-standing do not die easily.

Usually your life situation begins to change in this stage. There is the start of a great shift and adjustment, both in terms of external activities, but also in how you deal with and feel about relationships. Part of the difficulty is that you have lived a long life as a younger person, and the old ways of dealing with things is often difficult to let go of as things change. The opportunity to experiment more fully in life helps you to reassess yourself and what new way of relating and being suits you or is satisfying.

The psychiatrist Carl Jung and others such as Nietzsche developed a whole theory about this period of life that he called Individuation. Perhaps the influence of this began in the last periods during the forties, but becomes more marked now. As an individual we may come to recognise that our make-up is formed out of the collective experience of our family and the culture we have been exposed to. The question, "Who am I," leads us to look more fully into what makes us who we are. This awareness and the insight gained from it transforms us.

The change is that of becoming more fully independent of the forces that formed us. This means we create something new of who we are, and perhaps leave something of this new self in the world by what we do, create or live. Not every one undertakes yourself and what new way of relating and being suits you or is satisfying. The psychiatrist Carl Jung and others such as Nietzsche developed a whole theory about this period of life that he called Individuation. Perhaps the influence of this began in the last periods during the forties, but becomes more marked now.

As an individual we may come to recognise that our make-up is formed out of the collective experience of our family and the culture we have been exposed to. The question, "Who am I," leads us to look more fully into what makes us who we are. This awareness and the insight gained from it transform us. The change is that of becoming more fully independent of the forces that formed us. This means we create something new of who we are, and perhaps leave something of this new self in the world by what we do, create or live. Not every one undertakes

This is when we take an inventory of our life. It's a time of spiritual questioning and review of our life purpose. If we haven't successfully understood who we are by this stage and achieved our goals, then depression, moodiness and turmoil will plague both our waking life and our dreams

56-63 years
|
This period is often a time of inner tranquillity and acceptance. At peace with oneself and more accepting of where we are and what we have achieved marks this period. But many things that were lying unlived within you

might arise at this time, either as a form of unrest, or as directly living out those things that duty or work – or even self restraints – kept you from doing or being.

Usually your life situation begins to change in this stage. There is the start of a great shift and adjustment, both in terms of external activities, but also in how you deal with and feel about relationships. Part of the difficulty is that you have lived a long life as a younger person, and the old ways of dealing with things is often difficult to let go of as things change. The opportunity to experiment more fully in life helps you to reassess yourself and what new way of relating and being suits you or is satisfying.

The psychiatrist Carl Jung and others such as Nietzsche developed a whole theory about this period of life that he called Individuation. Perhaps the influence of this began in the last periods during the forties, but becomes more marked now. As an individual we may come to recognise that our make-up is formed out of the collective experience of our family and the culture we have been exposed to. The question, "Who am I," leads us to look more fully into what makes us who we are. This awareness and the insight gained from it transform us. The change is that of becoming more fully independent of the forces that formed us. This means we create something new of who we are, and perhaps leave something of this new self in the world by what we do, create or live. Not every one undertakes this diving into the depths of self to discover ones core being.

To quote from the website **Soul-Guidance**, "Individuation means that one becomes a person, an individual, a totally integrated personality. It is a process of self realization during which one integrates those contents of the psyche that have the ability to become conscious. It is a search for totality. It is an experience that could be formulated as the discovery of the divine in yourself, or the discovery of the totality of your Self. This does not always happen without pain, but it is necessary to accept many things that normally we would shy away from. Once a person has accepted the contents of his unconsciousness and has reached the goal of the individuation process, he is conscious of his relationships with everything that lives, with the entire cosmos."

]
63-70 years]

Now we have deeper acceptance and understanding of the people in our life. We appreciate the differences between us and our friends and look to the good rather than the bad in people. This is a period where our accumulated experience seeks new creative outlets.

A particularly noticeable process that occurs here is a conscious or unconscious sifting of life experience and moving toward what is the essence and best of what one has been learned from the years and experiences. Sometimes, if you can actually be aware of and work with this process, it leads to a sense of being lost or uncertain. By this is meant that for most of us external needs have dictated the direction of much that we have done or was needed of us. Now a great deal of this external pressure is removed. With its loss you realise that a great many choices or directions are open to you. It is like standing at cross roads with many directions. Which one do you want to take? Often it needs you to stand and observe before any direction from your own core wishes emerges. If during your life you have never worked at dealing with the difficulties and weaknesses or pains innate in you, then this period can lead to great confusion and the meeting of many shadows that you may not yet have developed the skills to deal with previously.

This is also a time in life when natural inner processes can lead you to a greater awareness of what lies beyond death. Things fall away naturally if you let them. A greater detachment from things of the world arises and this in itself is a foretaste of death in which you can let go of all that you have held on to.

70-77 years

If the issues met in the previous cycle have been dealt with, then there is a new awareness of the subtle sides of life, and a changed relationship with those you love or come in contact with. There is a greater unconditional love and acceptance. By this is meant that awareness of the depths and subtleties of ones own self are known more fully. If you are a person who has an active inner life, it can happen that the huge harvest of gathered life experience that was sifted and synthesised into clearer and more streamlined, or simpler concepts and meanings, is now expressed in your life and dealings with others. You may not be as powerful and active in the outer world, but you are gaining strength and effectiveness on people's inner life if you are still healthy. See **Intuition – Using It**

But such changes, as always, depend upon how well you have dealt with the problems, trauma as ability to grow during your life. If these are met, then this letter is an excellent example.

> Hi Tony- You probably won't remember me, I used to come to Combe Martin in the 1980s on Richard and Juliana's Intensives Psychotherapy

workshops… I remember fondly how we all enjoyed your and Hy's wonderful cooking!

Just wanted to say that as I approach old age (nearly 70), welcome changes are happening. Firstly, I'm accessing information I never knew I had, mainly evident in my enthusiasm for University Challenge on TV where I will often find the correct answers to questions on disparate subjects, they just seem to pop out of my head without consciously thinking which, in addition to surprising me, are sometimes not even guessed correctly by any of the eight panellists!

Secondly, synchronous-type occurrences are becoming more frequent. Things such as suddenly thinking of a friend I've not thought about for maybe weeks, only to have him or her then call or text me less than a minute later!

Also, the wider, world view you write of is becoming stronger in me, where I get a (intuitive) sense of the world at large, a strong feeling for the multitude and mass of humanity, and principally its collective suffering, which is a much more expansive experience than previously I've had most of my life ie my own small world and its restricted boundaries.

I've enjoyed, as I get older, the growth of my intuition, and celebrate its development in contrast to left-hemisphere mental (?) attributes such as intellect, objectivity, etc. I'm both fascinated and pleased to find your writings on these subjects, and more, on your website. It feels appropriate that I have come across your site at this time in my life.

Thanks for sharing all your wisdom on the site.

Best wishes. P

77-84 years onwards

During the three preceding periods a new self was developed. This emerged out of a summary and synthesis or all that you had lived. Perhaps, if you gave attention to your inner life, doorways of perception were opened through which you saw how your present life is a continuum of the long past, of ancestors and other influences. From this new self and widened perception you are acting and living in the world in a different way. The essence of the purpose, love, and ideas you lived by is given new expression. See **Ancestors**

As we have seen, the various physical changes have interacted with the spark of awareness lit at birth, causing changes in consciousness and attitude. Might we not speculate then, by saying that the biggest physical change of all-death – may be but a pre-requisite for yet another cycle of life, an initiation into an entirely new type of awareness? In fact it can happen that from the last cycle onwards, if you dare to experience your inner life reasonably fully, you will already have experienced what naked awareness is like or have penetrated what is called death in some way.

Breaking News – And Onwards Toward 100 Years

I am now 85, do not need glasses to see well, no need for hearing aid, my memory is still good, I am not troubled by arthritis, and I discovered a way of carrying on doing well.

In my seventies I had to be routinely medically examined. The doctor asked me how many medications I took. When I said, "I do not take any," he was silent for a while then more pointedly he said, "No, I need to know how many medications you need to take?

When I said again that I do not take any medications he left the room and came back with another doctor, perhaps his senior, and this one said to me in a serious tone. "I want to know how many medications you need to take daily." When I still said, "I do not need to take any," they finally left.

I can now understand that, because when I now go for my two medications due to having a serious stroke from which, due to the wonderful skill of the doctors I have recovered from, I see people in their sixties carrying out huge bags of medications.

How is it that I have survived so well despite having a very bad start? I know I have said some of this already, but it seems to need repeating. So my birth was in 1937 I was two months premature and born dead – not breathing – the doctor threw my lifeless body aside and told my mother that I would be a weak child and she could have more children. However, my grandmother witnessed this and carried my body off and bathed me in hot and cold water and got me breathing. I owe her my life she was my resurrection. The name of that resurrection was love. My grandmother had given birth to 13 children, some of whom died. I have a sense of her bearing an old and deep wisdom passed on through generations of women.

When I was born childbirth was surrounded by very different attitudes than exist today. The shadow of enormous mortality still fell over mothers and babies, and it influenced doctors. Antibiotics didn't exist. Infant care was not developed to the degree it is now. The doctor was telling my mother and grandmother a straightforward and accepted truth of the times – 'Why attempt to give life to this premature and tiny baby? It will be difficult to rear, more prone to illness, and it will be harder for it to cope with life. It isn't breathing at the moment, so forget it and try again for a healthy baby. Leave it'.

What I missed out of the story was that the gap between my thrown aside body and my grandmothers resurrection was that I had a near death experience. That because my lifeline, my umbilical cord, was cut early and I was not breathing, so the delay led to my sense of dying. I know many people cannot believe that a baby can remember such things. Well true they cannot remember as we do with words and images, but all life forms have enormous emotional responses and are known to experience a conditioned reflex. Whatever it was caused my baby self to remember, the experience of dying it left me with the desire to share the experience, to communicate to others about the wonder that we all are, about health of our body and the amazing world death reveals to us. See **The Baby Who Became Tony - What Happens When We Die?**

It took ages to realise that I was born a runt – a small or weak person – that could not function as normal healthy people can. I didn't realise the extent of its influence until I journeyed to Australia and had to have a full medical examination to enter. The woman doctor, a very efficient and straight-out person, asked me did I know I was born prematurely? I said I did and asked her how she knew. She said, look at the roof of your mouth, it shows your body never completed its growth.

 My mouth.

 A normal mouth. See **Mind of a New-born**

I wrote at the very beginning of this feature that, "We go through such enormous changes every day. Each of us is immersed in a 'river' of constant change. If you think about it, you have been carried, pushed, impelled by this current as you were moved through babyhood, childhood, teenage and adulthood, and there are more stages of growth beyond adulthood.

Maybe you have never given attention to that push that drives you onwards, except at this point in your life you may feel like getting rid of the damn thing driving you nearer to death. In fact you may be struggling to fight death and whatever moves you nearer to it. But I am not talking about the sicknesses many are trying to deal with at this period of life, I only am including those who are still afloat but don't wish to die because they see the sign of death has touched their body and it disturbs them. See **Are You Scared of Getting Healthy?**

What I am about to say may seem like I am hurrying you on your way to the end – but I tested it and the end seems further away. Your attitude of fighting off death is doing more to hurry you on. The reason is that the very force that has pushed you on through a whole life of experience is still doing its upmost to keep you going, and negative attitudes do not help. Yes we are going to die sometime, and maybe our attitudes and life style are not helping but working with the process of Life that grew you from the cell planted in your mother's womb and has done its best ever since is the very best option.

Something that works for me is to imagine myself being carried along by the 'river of constant change' mentioned, and not go fighting it through the fear of dying like Dylan Thomas did, "Do not go gentle into that good night".

Firstly the self-regulatory process underlying the fact that your body and mind are still functioning without your conscious effort, holds in it the continuous move to heal whatever hurts you experienced. It does this by pushing those experiences toward your conscious awareness in any way it can. The depressed feelings, psychosomatic body pains, irrational reaction we have to some situations, and of course the strange and sometimes frightening dreams we experience, are all ways this process attempts to make conscious what was hidden.

Secondly, the difficulties we need to deal with are all lined up just beneath conscious awareness, like a queue behind a closed door waiting to come through.

Thirdly, the reason things do not surface, become known and resolved is because we resist them. These resistances are obvious and need to be meet for healing to take place. Dreamers wake with terror from a nightmare for instance and desire nothing more than to blot it out from their feelings. The nightmare is an attempt to make conscious the intense feelings from a trauma, but we resist this because we have not learned the ability to witness such feelings and personal emotions without fear.

Another resistance is the automatic withdrawal from pain. Just as we automatically draw our hand away from a hot surface, so we draw our awareness away from a painful memory. The methods we use are many – using redirected attention, as when we rush to entertainment, alcohol, talking with friends, nicotine, breath holding, and so on.

Such resistances are the main reason we do not find healing through dreaming, even though dreams are constantly trying to heal us. Of course another one seen in massive number of dreams is fear. Fear acts just like pain to make us avoid/resist the action of dreams.

So recognising these processes in oneself is the first step to self-discovery

An example of this from the life of Norman Cousins, who was at one time the editor of Newsweek in America. At a time when he faced enormous stress and became seriously ill and was hospitalised. In the hospital his condition degenerated. One day one of the doctors on his case left a note for a colleague who was to examine him later. Being puzzled and troubled about his condition Norman opened the envelope and read the note. It said, I feel we are losing Norman.

This was naturally a great shock to him. He had not realised how serious his illness was. Understanding now that the doctors felt doubt about being able to help him, he made efforts to help himself. He carefully considered his activities during the last year. It was obvious as he reviewed them that the year had been particularly stressful, culminating in the tension in Moscow. So his next step was to ask his wife to bring him books about stress. As he read through them he saw that in essence they were saying that during stress our glandular system produces substances which enter the bloodstream and have a destructive effect on the body and its health. During periods of pleasure and relaxation the glandular system produces substances which enter the bloodstream and are constructive to the body and health.

Norman was then faced with an enormous decision – whether to take his health into his own hands. He decided yes and had himself discharged from hospital and taken to a hotel apartment. He was in such physical pain he could hardly move, so had to remain almost immobile. He had friends set up a cine film projector and screen near his bed, and had them show all his favourite comedy films. In his bed he chuckled, laughed and roared at the antics of the great film comedians, and he discovered that for every hour of laughter, he had an hour of release from pain.

Over the following days his condition radically improved. That is to say, even such fundamental things as the condition of blood, which was part of his illness, changed for the better. During this period he also took very high doses of Vitamin C, which he had been told aided healthy collagen formation in the body. In two weeks he was back at work, his pain and illness gone. He had fought the battle of physical pain and negative emotions and had won.

Do You Want To Take Your Health Into Your Own Hands?
Well, maybe not entirely, but like Norman there are things you can do.

Is it not a sobering thought to realise that more and more of our race, through its growing diet of chemicals and manufactured food, are being born with malformations? Joan Grant, during an archaeological dig in the Middle

East, collected forty sets of teeth. She says that there were 'children's teeth, middle-aged teeth, teeth of men who were so old that the surface of the molars was ground almost smooth and in none of the forty sets she collected was there a single decayed tooth, nor a jaw abscess, nor a wisdom tooth that had not grown in exact alignment with the rest.'

But it is not simply malformations but serious illnesses that are the result of our modern diet. So, in today's world many, many of us are slowly creating illness in our bodies through our daily diet. For example Dr. Noakes made a statement to the public in South Africa that the 'normal' foods they ate are the cause of the many illnesses they experience. The normal foods are those that are manufactured that we eat. The main ones are all products made with white flour and white rice and the use of white sugar, all of which are highly manufactured and is no longer a natural food. This includes many of our staple dietary floods such white bread, cakes of all sorts, biscuits, pizzas, pancakes, white sugar, and white rice.

The main damage the 'normal' diet does is to deny us enough of certain vitamins such as the B group, vitamins A, E, D and sometimes C which were usually provided by eating enormous amounts vegetables, whole grains as in wholegrain wheat and rice and being exposed to sunlight. So it is wise to take a multi vitamin and mineral tablet daily as a precaution. Without the B vitamin group people suffer swollen ankles, white hair in their late sixties, neuralgic pain, especially back of the legs. But also many of us lack the enormous protection given by vitamin A, D and E. An example was that while in Australia I learnt that many native Australian's who live in the centre of the land suffer badly from eye conditions, but those aboriginals who lived on the coast had perfect eyes. The reason being that on the coast they ate oily fish rich in Vitamin A. So it is also wise to regularly take this perhaps as Cod Liver Oil.

My son Leon who is a graduate of Cambridge University, UK, has made a study of how one can prolong ones life. His suggestions are to take these capsules, they are not medications but life enhancers.

Fisetin - Advanced Pterostilbene - Trans Resveratrol – NMN - Tru Niagen – Turkey Tail – Lions Mane

They are all available on Amazon or any good health store. See Defeating Alzheimer's

Sex

Yes, as you age many will find their sexual ability to slowly disappear. I am 85 now and find it is a wonderful freedom to not be under the influence of having all the time to want or seek out a sexual partner. I know many people do not cherish such freedom and fight to keep it active by drugs etc. Personally being without the huge waves of hormonal sexual impulse I see my sense of beauty for all living things has grown tremendously. Something I have realised through this is that 'falling in love' as it is called is purely a glandular event. It fires enormous stimulus to our emotions and leads us to see certain men or women as wonderful. Of course that is nature at work in us, and if the urge is traumatised it leads to neurotic behaviour. Understanding that we can work with instead of being dominated by it.

Who Am I Now

I am an old guy of 85. I don't mind looking old like many men and women who seem to have mask like faces without any wrinkles or bags under their eyes. I even have difficulty walking, after effects of the major stroke I experienced. I also had a bad time with my prostate. It

wasn't cancerous, it had got so big I couldn't pee. Without modern medicine it would have killed my body.

But years earlier I felt death was coming for me - but if that was it now coming at the age of 13 making noises in my chest, I was going to squirm as hard as I could to break loose. But it wasn't easy. Soon afterwards I discovered I'd got a pain in my chest just about where my heart was. Things began to look bad, I thought. At thirteen I was too young to die. Well, I would go to the doctor. My female doctor told me in no uncertain terms that I was a hypochondriac. I didn't know what a hypochondriac was, but she hadn't acted as if it were not any immediate threat. Maybe it was a slower death than heart attack. When I got home the dictionary told me the problem was not in the body but in the soul. So? Well, if I could develop a bigger chest through deep breathing maybe there were things people did to their soul to liven it up. If there were, I would do it.

In fact I did, for in 1978 I had my first experience of enlightenment. It happened because I had torn myself apart trying to heal myself and had suddenly realised that nothing I had done with all my efforts had any effect - so I was lost and gave up completely. To quote: "During the past months I have been in such turmoil I have feared madness - a life of conflict - unknown years of pain. Then suddenly, two days ago I found peace. The only thing I can see as the turning point is complete surrender, a total giving up. Then it was like an experience of enlightenment."

It occurred because for two days I used the Enlightenment Intensive method. The building that I was in was full of people on social security, babies running around the place, somebody playing a mall grand piano continuously. Outside dogs were barking. There were sounds of people and birds along with traffic noise. I began to hear all these sounds not as separate, but as different parts of one great and wonderful whole. And as I listened I began to hear what it was telling me. I realised it had always been speaking to me, but I had never heard it before, all Life was expressing as One Great Voice."

I heard it here this afternoon,
One voice sang through them all,
Collecting all the sounds of Life,
Into one vibrant call.

Once heard the Voice in you works like yeast, slowly changing your very person. Now I am that changed Person who has lived through what others call grief, heart break, awful sickness - yet each so called tragedy only showed me wonders, for me there was no final ending of death. for as my parents died, my eyes were opened, and I saw life and death are bound together, heartbreak was felt and transcended. Here I am at 85 and I don't need glasses or hearing aids for I have touched the Wonder. See https://dreamhawk.com/dream.../psychological-vomiting/

Tony Through The Ages
Tony as a teenager at seventeen - then in his seventies - and now in his eighties

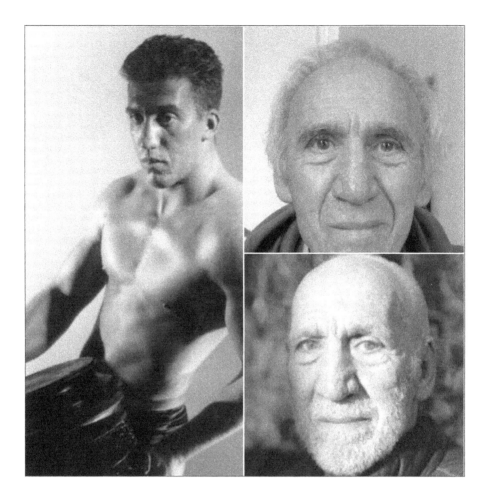

Printed in the USA
CPSIA information can be obtained
at www.ICGtesting.com
LVHW041045160424
777553LV00032B/784